OTHER GOLF GIFTBOOKS BY EXLEY:

Golf Quotations   The Fanatic's Guide to Golf
Golf a Celebration   The Crazy World of Golf
Golf Score Book   The Love of Golf Address Book
A Round of Golf Jokes   The World's Greatest Golf Cartoons
The Golfer's Address Book

Published simultaneously in 1995 by Exley Publications
in Great Britain, and Exley Giftbooks in the USA.

12 11 10 9 8 7 6 5

Selection and arrangement © Helen Exley 1995
The moral right of the author has been asserted.

ISBN 1-85015-985-8
        1-86187-018-3 (Personalised edition)

Words and pictures selected by Helen Exley.
Picture research by Image Select International.
Typeset by Delta, Watford.
Printed at Oriental Press, UAE.

Thanks to Margaret Montgomery for her help with text research.

"Golf is a good walk spoiled" – Mark Twain

Exley Publications Ltd, 16 Chalk Hill, Watford, Herts WD1 4BN, UK.
Exley Publications LLC, 232 Madison Avenue, Suite 1206, NY 10016, USA.

GOLF
A GOOD WALK SPOILED

HUMOROUS WORDS AND PAINTINGS
SELECTED BY
HELEN EXLEY

EXLEY
NEW YORK • WATFORD, UK

The protocol of Golf is subtle. It involves much more than being able to mark down on the score card an 8 that looks like a 3. The Golfer, like the Hindu mystic, must focus an enormous amount of concentration in order to transcend reality. This means that when one's opponent is into his backswing, one should not pass wind. It also precludes coughing, sneezing, wheezing, snapping bubble gum, tummy rumbles, and reciting the Gettysburg address. The Golfer addressing the ball is aware not only of such sounds but of where his companions are standing. If the rest of his foursome are bunched directly behind his ball, or assume the foetal position with their backs to the tee, the Golfer is reminded that his drive tends to be erratic. More cruel yet is for his opponent to stand directly in the projected line of flight, as the safest place to be.

ERIC NICOL AND DAVE MORE, *FROM "GOLF. THE AGONY AND THE ECSTASY"*

If you can keep your head when the wheels come off your game, you need a new head.

FROM "GOLF FOREVER, WORK WHENEVER",
COMP. MICHAEL RYAN

Golf is a game where guts, stick-to-itiveness and blind devotion will always net you absolutely nothing but an ulcer.

TOMMY BOLT,
FROM "GOLF FOREVER, WORK WHENEVER"
COMP. MICHAEL RYAN

The least thing upsets him on the links. He misses short putts because of the uproar of the butterflies in the adjoining meadows.

P.G.WODEHOUSE

Be funny on a golf course? Do I kid my best friend's mother about her heart condition?

PHIL SILVERS

Golf is like a love affair: if you don't take it seriously, it's no fun; if you do take it seriously, it breaks your heart.

ARNOLD DALY

I guess there is nothing that will get your mind off everything like golf. I have never been depressed enough to take up the game but they say you get so sore at yourself, you forget to hate your enemies.

WILL ROGERS

You can be black or white, introvert or extrovert, male or female, but to my mind there are only two types of people in the world: golfers and non-golfers. Once bitten, it is akin to having your neck punctured in Transylvania – there is no known antidote.

MARTIN JOHNSON, *FROM "ONE OVER PAR"*

My car absolutely will not run unless my golf clubs are in the trunk.

BRUCE BERLET

[Golfaholics] are never content when the round is over. They want "just one more" hole to take away the bad taste of the previous 18. Or they insist on working out their miseries on the putting green hour after hour, oblivious to other plans for the afternoon – like a wedding. Theirs.

MARK OMAN, *FROM "PORTRAIT OF A GOLFAHOLIC"*

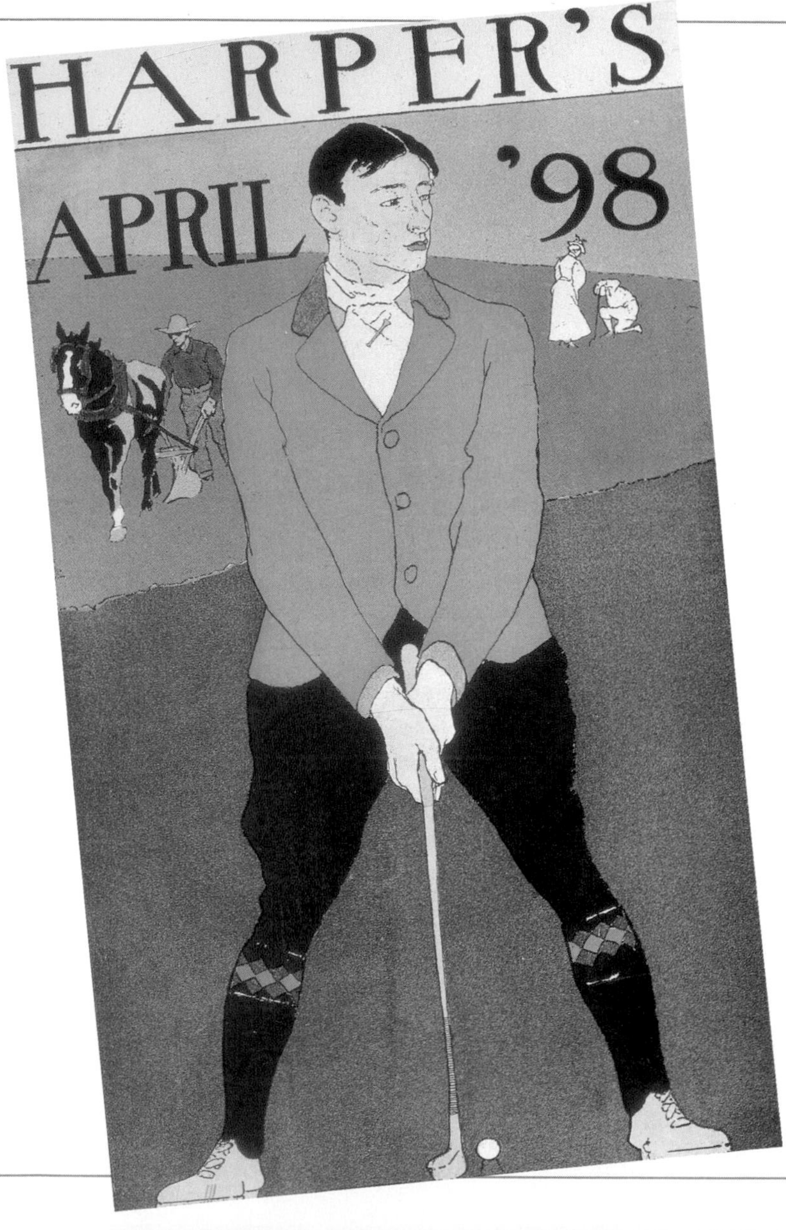
HARPER'S
APRIL
'98

While it is true that some amateur golfers are unwittingly or unwillingly duped, badgered, or coerced into playing a round of golf, an incredible 97 percent of the dummies actually report to the first tee on a *voluntary* basis!

This is a dumbfounding statistic in light of the fact that the undertaking will result in the complete destruction of the golfing novice's carefully and expensively groomed facade as a competent golfer.

The reason for this illogical behavior apparently stems from the amateur golfer's nasty habit of falling prey to the very illusion so painstakingly created. Caught up in the splendor of his dazzling new golfing wardrobe and weaponry, the golfing rookie comes to the utterly absurd conclusion that he can actually play the !!#*#!* game!

GEOFF HOWSON,
FROM "GOLF: HOW TO LOOK GOOD WHEN YOU'RE NOT"

GOLF IS A TERRIBLE, HOPELESS ADDICTION, IT SEEMS: IT MAKES ITS DEVOTEES WILLING TO TRUDGE MILES IN ANY MANNER OF WEATHER, LUGGING A HUGE, INCOMMODIOUS AND APPALLINGLY HEAVY BAG WITH THEM, IN PURSUIT OF A TINY AND FANTASTICALLY EXPENSIVE BALL, IN A FANATICAL ATTEMPT TO DIRECT IT INTO A HOLE THE SIZE OF A BEER GLASS HALF A MILE AWAY. IF ANYTHING COULD BE BETTER CALCULATED TO CONVINCE ONE OF THE ESSENTIAL LUNACY OF THE HUMAN RACE, I HAVEN'T FOUND IT. AND YET IT GIVES ONE A BREATH OF HOPE WHEN ONE PERCEIVES THAT ITS MOST ARDENT DEVOTEES ARE, SOMEWHERE VERY DEEP INSIDE, FULLY AWARE OF THE ABSURDITY OF THEIR CONSUMING PASSION.

MIKE SEABROOK,
FROM "ONE OVER PAR"

Golf, you see, is not a game, but an addiction that draws
unassuming clods deeper and deeper into its seductive web.
Like any worthwhile bad habit, the more one plays the game,
the more one wants to play the game, and at four to five hours
per round of golf severe marital distress can result from the
addiction unless one's spouse has also been afflicted.

Financial ruin is a distinct possibility due to the expensive
nature of the sport, and of course moral corruption is
completely unavoidable thanks to the incessant temptations to
gamble, curse, lie and cheat.

The most terrifying aspect of the affliction, however, is that it
can maim, and even kill! Hypertension, heart disease, stroke
and temporary insanity are but a few possible by-products of
one's continuous frustration over attempting to properly hit a
bloody little golf ball.

In conclusion, then, I would suggest that the would-be golfer
consider this last piece of advice first!

NEVER TAKE UP THE GAME OF GOLF.

GEOFF HOWSON,
FROM "GOLF: HOW TO LOOK GOOD WHEN YOU'RE NOT"

WHY DO WE PLAY THIS WRETCHED GAME?

We are all such wretched optimists...

Despite all our experience to the contrary, there we stand once again at the first tee. We have before us a strange shaped weapon with which we try, against all odds, to hit a small hard object an incredibly long way into a small round hole. It doesn't matter what the weather throws at us. If there's snow on the ground we'll use red golf balls. If it's sleeting with rain and all other sane human beings are gathered around hearth and home we're still there.

As we stand musing at the first tee, we know anything can happen. And probably will. There's a goodly chance the ball will disappear forever in some hazard far down the green. We may hook it to the left. We may slice it to the right. We may top the ball, or murder the groundsman's turf. We may even drive the ball straight through the club secretary's office windows. The one thing we can be sure of is that there is a fairly remote chance of the wretched thing going where it's supposed to go, straight down the middle of the fairway.

We've got to be doing all this to prove something. But what? That we have uncanny skill and judgment? That we are of a calm, saintly, unruffable disposition? That we have a masterly command of the tactics of life?

Golfers sometimes muse that they are there to master the pressures the game exerts on them. But then there wouldn't be any pressure in the first place if they didn't stand there trying to master the pressures would there?

RICHARD ALAN

Golfaholism is only now coming into its own as a major sports affliction. It is estimated that nearly 15 million people in the United States alone suffer from problem golfing and golfaholism. This group includes both men and women of all ages. Today, throughout the world, golfaholism is responsible for untold broken clubs, abused caddies, and battered golf carts. The price for such carnage is high. Golfaholism costs its afflictees millions of dollars every year in the compulsive pursuit of the latest methodology and equipment designed to aid and abet golfaholics in their addiction to the impossible dream of

conquering the maddening game.... Even today many casual golfers refuse to believe that golf is a drug. In the beginning it works mostly as a stimulant – players get excited by the prospect of a game and look forward to teeing off. But as they get deeper into dependence, golf becomes a major depressant. Somehow the afflictees' golfing never seems to live up to expectation.

Like other forms of compulsive behavior, for true golfaholics even nine holes are more than they should attempt, yet 18 holes are not enough to satisfy their insatiable craving for humiliation and self-abuse.

The affliction is of such an insidious nature that afflictees often suffer vivid and detailed hallucinations of incredible shot-making exploits – of course these are rarely, if ever, seen by the other golfaholics in the foursome.

As the torment spreads deeper into the mind and putting stroke, these grand illusions are slowly replaced by lapses in memory, sometimes of an entire round of golf.

From here, it is only a matter of time before functional disintegration and paranoia take over and the golfaholic's handicap becomes totally out of control.

MARK OMAN,
FROM "PORTRAIT OF A GOLFAHOLIC"

Willis' Rule of Golf: You can't lose an old golf ball.

JOHN WILLIS

Putt in haste and repent at leisure.

GERALD BATCHELOR

A ball will always travel farthest when hit in the wrong direction.

FROM "GOLF FOREVER, WORK WHENEVER", COMP. MICHAEL RYAN

The longer the grass, the shorter the temper.

GERALD BATCHELOR

If you ever par the first three holes, you'll have a 20-minute wait on the fourth tee.

FROM "GOLF FOREVER, WORK WHENEVER", COMP. MICHAEL RYAN

The number of tees in your bag is always less than 3 or more than 600.

FROM "GOLF FOREVER, WORK WHENEVER",
COMP. MICHAEL RYAN

All holes are blind to those who cannot play.

GERALD BATCHELOR

It is a law of nature that everybody plays a hole badly when going through.

BERNARD DARWIN

The greater the bet, the longer the short putts become.

FROM "GOLF FOREVER, WORK WHENEVER",
COMP. MICHAEL RYAN

He's an unwise pro that beats his only pupil.

GERALD BATCHELOR

THE MOST EXQUISITELY SATISFYING ACT IN THE WORLD OF GOLF IS

THAT OF THROWING A CLUB. THE FULL BACKSWING, THE DELAYED

WRIST ACTION, THE FLOWING FOLLOW-THROUGH, FOLLOWED BY THAT

UNIQUE WHIRRING SOUND, REMINISCENT ONLY OF A PASSING FLOCK OF

STARLINGS, ARE WITHOUT PARALLEL IN SPORT.

HENRY LONGHURST

I GET UPSET OVER A BAD SHOT JUST LIKE ANYONE ELSE. BUT IT'S

SILLY TO LET THE GAME GET TO YOU. WHEN I MISS A SHOT I JUST

THINK WHAT A BEAUTIFUL DAY IT IS. AND WHAT PURE FRESH AIR I'M

BREATHING. THEN I TAKE A DEEP BREATH. I HAVE TO DO THAT. THAT'S

WHAT GIVES ME THE STRENGTH TO BREAK THE CLUB.

BOB HOPE, *FROM "CONFESSIONS OF A HOOKER"*

COMPETITIVE GOLF IS PLAYED MAINLY ON A FIVE-AND-A-HALF-INCH COURSE, THE SPACE BETWEEN YOUR EARS.

BOBBY JONES

The golfer has more enemies than any other athlete. He has 14 clubs in his bag, all of them different; 18 holes to play, all of them different, every week; and all around him are sand, trees, grass, water, wind, and 143 other players. In addition, the game is 50 percent mental, so his biggest enemy is himself.

DAN JENKINS, *FROM "SPORTS ILLUSTRATED" 1982*

… the greatest enemy of the lot, in golf, it seems to me, watching enthralled from my armchair…is the player himself. Every action he makes is a potential disaster waiting to happen. The weather and the lie he cannot help. His method of countering them, he can. It's all down to him. In this sense, it seems to me that golf is an even higher form of self-immolation than snooker. In snooker there is no weather, and no lie of the land. There is the lie of the balls, but that is within the power of the player to make favourable or not. Golf is the only game that pits the player against an opponent, the weather, the minutest details of a large chunk of local topography and his own nervous system, all at the same time.

MIKE SEABROOK, *FROM "ONE OVER PAR"*

The Golfer who owns a complete set of clubs ... is universally recognized as a person accustomed to making decisions. Each decision may take long enough to be mistaken for catalepsy, but this is what makes Golf one of the great contemplative religions. Other sport is mere action. Impulse is rife. If the player makes a bad judgement in propelling the ball or puck, in a matter of seconds he has the chance to make another bad judgement. Golf, in contrast, thanks to the plenitude of sources for nothing happening, is a kind of inspired inertia. All but the blind or importunate see a poetry in the slow withdrawal of the club from the bag, the gazing at the horizon, the return of the club to the bag, the withdrawal of another club from the bag... There is good reason why the senior executive feels free to practise chip shots in his office. His associates recognize that it is not just play but preparation for corporate life, in which poise counts for more than action.

ERIC NICOL AND DAVE MORE, *FROM "GOLF. THE AGONY AND THE ECSTASY"*

GOLF ETIQUETTE

ALMOST AS IMPORTANT AS KNOWING THE RULES IS KNOWING HOW TO "BEHAVE" ON THE COURSE. HERE ARE SOME COURTESIES TO REMEMBER.

Repair and replace divots, glue branches back on trees, repair benches smashed by reckless practice swings or tantrums, and rake sand traps, but not while others are in them.

Never drive an electric cart into a sand trap, onto a green, too close to a water hazard, or over an opponent.

If, while you're searching for a ball, players behind you are striking up poker games or betting who can balance a ball on their 9 iron longer, then it's time to let them play through.

Try not to create new lavatories on the course, especially in the cup, sand traps, or water hazards.

Never realign sprinkler heads to face your opponents.

When a player is putting you should not stand directly behind the hole or with one foot covering the cup.

Never confuse the following foursome by sticking the flagstick into a part of the green other than the cup.

Never toss a golf club, bag, or caddie onto the putting green.

*Try not to drive over an opponent's ball with your cart or wedge
it into the ground with the heel of your shoe.*

*Keep the sound from the baseball game on your portable
TV turned down.*

RICHARD MINTZER, *FROM "THE UNOFFICIAL GOLFER'S HANDBOOK"*

An English doctor in Bombay on a trip was called in to perform an emergency operation on a Maharajah, and made a masterly job of it. "You have saved my life", said the prince when he was convalescent, "whatever you want shall be yours."

"Oh, it was nothing really", protested the surgeon.

"I insist", said His Highness.

"Well, I would go for a new matched set of golf clubs."

"It is done."

The surgeon returned to England and forgot about the matter until, six weeks later, he received this cable: "Have your fourteen clubs but regret all not matched Stop Three are without swimming pools Stop."

TOM SCOTT AND GEOFFREY COUSINS, *FROM "THE WIT OF GOLF"*

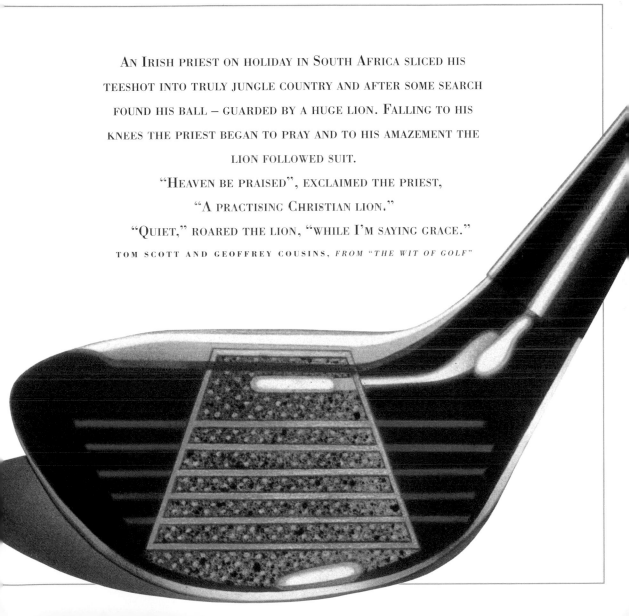

AN IRISH PRIEST ON HOLIDAY IN SOUTH AFRICA SLICED HIS
TEESHOT INTO TRULY JUNGLE COUNTRY AND AFTER SOME SEARCH
FOUND HIS BALL — GUARDED BY A HUGE LION. FALLING TO HIS
KNEES THE PRIEST BEGAN TO PRAY AND TO HIS AMAZEMENT THE
LION FOLLOWED SUIT.
"HEAVEN BE PRAISED", EXCLAIMED THE PRIEST,
"A PRACTISING CHRISTIAN LION."
"QUIET," ROARED THE LION, "WHILE I'M SAYING GRACE."
TOM SCOTT AND GEOFFREY COUSINS, *FROM "THE WIT OF GOLF"*

Once in Scotland I played with the most
fanatical golfer I've ever met. We were just
teeing off on the 15th where the green lies next
to the main road. He was in the middle of his
backswing when a row of funeral cars came
past. He stopped, took off his cap, held it over
his heart and bowed his head. I was impressed.
I said, "You're a man who shows real respect
for the deceased." He said, "It's only fair.
She was a good wife to me for 37 years."

BOB MONKHOUSE

Mad Mac, for many years Max Faulkner's caddie, had another client who looked after him very well. A quiet man, a bit of a recluse, he liked his round of golf, but preferred to play with imaginary clubs – which Mad Mac of course carried for him.

The fellow would go through the motions, with Mac supplying the sound effects, the swishing of the club, the crack as it hit the ball. Then Mac would cry: "Oh, lovely shot, sir. Two hundred and twenty yards, just down the middle of the fairway."

Then Mac hoisted the imaginary bag onto his shoulder and they'd walk down the fairway. Mac handed his client a 7-iron, and watched him make his stroke. "Whaackkk. Oh, well done, sir."

One day they were going round, and had got to the 11th when the people behind them caught up. They were fascinated by what they'd been seeing. One of them asked Mac what on earth was going on, imaginary clubs, swiping at thin air and so on.

"Ssshh," said Mac, a finger to his lips. "Don't you disturb him. He's four under par and that's the best he's ever done on this course."

"What do you mean?" cried the fellow. "It's crazy. You've got no clubs, no ball, what's it all for?"

"I'm not sure myself," said Mac. "Not a word to him, though. He hasn't got a car either, but he gives me a tenner a week to keep it clean."

PETER ALLISS, *FROM "BEDSIDE GOLF"*

Golf increases the blood pressure, ruins the disposition, spoils the digestion, induces neurasthenia, hurts the eyes, callouses the hands, ties kinks in the nervous system, debauches the morals, drives men to drink or homicide, breaks up the family, turns the ductless glands into internal warts, corrodes the pneumogastric nerve, breaks off the edges of the vertebrae, induces spinal meningitis and progressive mendacity, and starts angina pectoris.

DR. A.S. LAMB

Bob Hope tells the story that his doctor told him he was overworked for a man in his eighties and needed a complete rest – and that included giving up golf. Hope decided to give up his doctor instead. He tried a second opinion and a third, and on the fourth try he found a doctor who told him he could play eighteen holes whenever he felt like it. Hope says he actually hugged the man and said, "Thanks, doc, just for that I'll remember you in my will." And the doctor said, "In that case, play thirty-six."

BOB MONKHOUSE

Your financial cost can best be figured out when you realize that if you were to devote the same time and energy to business instead of golf, you would be a millionaire in approximately six weeks.

BUDDY HACKETT

One philosopher had this to say about golf: "By the time you can afford to lose a ball, you can't hit it that far."

VIC FREDERICKS, *FROM "FOR GOLFERS ONLY"*

Golf is a form of work made expensive enough for a rich man to enjoy it. It is physical and mental exertion made attractive by the fact that you have to dress for it in a $350,000 clubhouse.

The game is played on carefully selected grass with little white balls and as many clubs as the player can afford. These balls cost from 75c to $1.25 and it is possible to support a family of 10 people (all adults) for five months on the money represented by the balls lost by some golfers in a single afternoon.

A golf course has 18 holes, 17 of which are unnecessary and put in to make the game harder. A "hole" is a tin cup in the center of a "green".

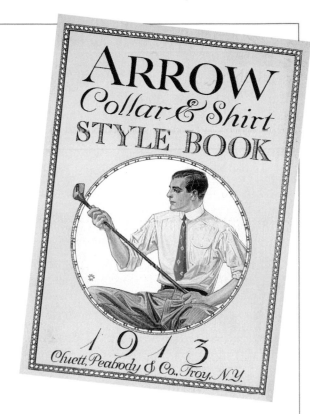

A "green" is a small parcel of grass costing about $2.98 a blade, and usually situated between a brook and a couple of apple trees or a lot of "unfinished excavation".

ANONYMOUS

YOU KNOW YOU'RE HAVING A BAD DAY WHEN...

– You run over your own foot with your electric cart.

– Other golfers have nicknamed you "Shank".

– Your shoes are filled with enough sand to open your own private beach club.

– You've lifted your head so often you have a crick in your neck.

– The rest of your foursome huddles behind a bench as you tee off.

– Your tee-off time for tomorrow has been revoked.

– Your club membership has been revoked.

– Your woods are too embarrassed to come out of the bag.

– The course pro introduces you to a tennis instructor.

– The course superintendent threatens you with legal action.

– Birds flying south readjust their flight pattern to let you hit.

– People are offering you good prices for your clubs.

– Between the 9th and 10th holes, life insurance salesmen approach you in the clubhouse.

RICHARD MINTZER, *FROM "THE UNOFFICIAL GOLFER'S HANDBOOK"*

Doubtless the first man or woman to hit a pebble with a stick did so without thinking how it was done, but after a while, he or she would begin to wonder why the pebble could not be hit straighter and further. Other hitters would gather round and exchange views and in between inventing the wheel and discovering fire, would draw various conclusions as to what movement would make for straight and powerful hitting of the pebble. It would be at this juncture that the pebble hitters would get the first inkling that their physiology was ill-designed for their requirements.

Today's golfer, the modern equivalent of those ancient pebble hitters, faces much the same problem. God has persisted with His design and we find ourselves embarking on the job of hitting a golf ball still stuck with those symmetrical arms, legs, eyes, muscles and joints. Thus equipped, we find that to make an efficient pass at the ball we have to make one arm longer than the other, one leg shorter than the other, stiffen the joints in one arm, concave our chests and from the tip of this contorted structure peer at the ball through one eye like a Cyclops.

CHRIS PLUMRIDGE, *FROM "ALMOST STRAIGHT DOWN THE MIDDLE"*

Golf clubhouse employees are a carefully trained lot. Take this locker-room boy for instance. One Saturday evening he answered the telephone and a female voice said, "Is my husband there?" The boy answered promptly, "No Ma'am."

"How can you say he isn't there before I even tell you who I am?"

"Don' make no difference, Lady. They ain't never nobody's husband here."

SEYMOUR DUNN, *FROM "THE COMPLETE GOLF JOKE BOOK"*

When you return home after a day's golf, don't run away with the idea that your wife and family are interested in doing things. Tell them nothing, for if you do, in the exaggerated style of all golfers, they will be so proud of you that they will want to see you perform at the earliest opportunity – and remember, a novice playing before the critical gaze of his own family, who have been led to expect great things, is one of the most pitiable things in the whole world of sport.

"Did you hit it on the top purposely, father?" is a remark that requires a lot of answering; and should you miss a foot putt, as likely as not your youngest will show you how to do it with a walking-stick. Therefore, do not pose as a champion before your own family.

HARRY FULFORD

I loathe golf advice. I loathe golf pros. Everyone suggests: straighten this, twist that, look down, relax, swing, move your thumb up, move your thumb down. And all of this because the course designers and the pros are in collusion. One is paid to drive you mad by making the course impossible. The other is paid to drive you mad teaching you how to overcome the obstacles that shouldn't have been there in the first place.

Relax. Roll with the system. Book in for another 10 lessons.

You're nearly there...

HELEN RICHARDS

My golf pro wouldn't tell me to visualize my shots if he could see what I see.

FROM "GOLF FOREVER, WORK WHENEVER",
COMP. MICHAEL RYAN

There is no movement in the golf swing so difficult that it cannot be made even more difficult by careful study and difficult practice.

FROM "GOLF FOREVER, WORK WHENEVER",
COMP. MICHAEL RYAN

Being a left-handed golfer is a big advantage. No one knows enough about your swing to mess you up with advice.

BOB CHARLES

No one who ever had lessons would have a swing like mine.

LEE TREVINO

Golfaholics... have blackouts, can't remember kicking their ball out from behind the tree. They'll tell family, friends, and neighbors about their "three" on the tough ninth hole, but forget completely about their "nine" on the easy third hole. This type of memory lapse has been diagnosed incorrectly as "hysterical amnesia," though in fact, only when they remember the nine shots do they get hysterical.

MARK OMAN,
FROM "PORTRAIT OF A GOLFAHOLIC"

SONGS *from*
"THE GOLF SPECIAL"
A Musical Comedy Presented by
The Standard Club Amateurs
AT THE ANNUAL
**WASHINGTON'S BIRTHDAY
CELEBRATION**
SATURDAY EVE., FEB. 20th, 1909

The newly converted golf enthusiast was introducing his bride to the game. He had expounded at great length on what a fine exercise golf was, the beauty of the countryside and the joy of being "out in the open."

On the first tee he prepared to give his first demonstration of the game itself. Taking his stance he swung hard – and missed. Embarrassed, he re-organised his stance and swung again. Again he missed. His third effort was also a wiff.

At this point his bride asked innocently, "George, I can see that golf is a fine exercise. *But what's the little ball for?*"

SEYMOUR DUNN, *FROM "THE COMPLETE GOLF JOKE BOOK"*

I don't care to join any club that's prepared to have me as a member.

GROUCHO MARX

People who don't play golf don't know what they're missing. But golfers do. The ball!

SEYMOUR DUNN, *FROM "THE COMPLETE GOLF JOKE BOOK"*

The Earl of Wemyss was on a Fife course not long ago, accompanied by an old caddie. His lordship got his ball on one occasion so near the hole that to play it was, as it appeared to him, superfluous. So he simply tipped it in off the toe of his boot. The caddie revolted at once, threw down the clubs, and looked horrified. When he found words to speak it was to say, "Dammit, ma lord, gowf's gowf."

MILES BANTOCK

"If your ball lands within a club's length of a rattlesnake you are allowed to move the ball."

LOCAL RULE AT THE GLEN CANYON COURSE IN ARIZONA

"After all, golf is only a game," said Millicent. Women say these things without thinking. It does not mean that there is any kink in their character. They simply don't realize what they are saying.

P.G. WODEHOUSE

Golf is a sport, a bloodless sport, if you don't count ulcers.

DICK SCHAPP

If a ball comes to rest in dangerous proximity to a hippopotamus or crocodile, another ball may be dropped at a safe distance, no nearer the hole, without penalty.

NYANZA CLUB RULE, 1950

At Jinja there is both hotel and golf course. The latter is, I believe, the only course in the world which posts a special rule that the player may remove his ball from hippopotamus footprints.

EVELYN WAUGH

I may be the only golfer never to have broken a single putter,
if you don't count the one I twisted into a loop and
threw into a bush.

THOMAS BOSWELL

You would like to gather up several holes from Prestwick and
mail them to your top ten enemies.

DAN JENKINS

"You wanna go and hit that now, while you're still mad?"

LEE TREVINO, *to an opponent who had just putted five feet past the hole*

Always throw clubs ahead of you. That way you don't have
to waste energy going back to pick them up.

TOMMY BOLT

Golfer Tommy Bolt is known for his sweet swing and foul
temper. While giving a clinic to a group of amateurs,
Bolt tried to show his softer side by involving his
fourteen-year-old son in the lesson.
"Show the nice folks what I taught you," said Bolt. His son
obediently took a nine iron, cursed, and hurled it into the sky.

ANONYMOUS

The niblick, with its heavy head of iron, a capital club for
knocking down solicitors.

ANONYMOUS

A cardinal rule for the club breaker is never to break your
putter and driver in the same match or you are dead.

TOMMY BOLT

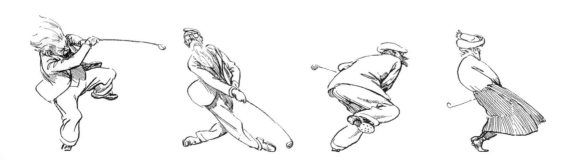

The following chart will put matters in their true perspective:

HANDICAP	OFFICIAL DEFINITION	TRUTH
40	*A human rat who should be thrown off every course*	The backbone of the game. A splendid fellow who will give you an enjoyable round and who undoubtedly has that generous interpretation of the rules which is the mark of the gentleman
35	*Does not exist*	The ideal opponent. Always a tough game. Probably a golf writer
24	*Rabbit*	Rather a tiger. Avoid him. Although ten strokes better than you he won't concede any. May be pedantic about little things like not counting air shots
19	*Rabbit*	A leopard. This man may actually have won a competition
12	*A mere handicap player*	A positive jaguar. But don't worry, he wouldn't want to play with you.
Scratch	*A useful golfer*	These people do not exist outside television screens

MICHAEL GREEN, *FROM "THE ART OF COARSE GOLF"*

Many clergymen in Scotland, in the early days of the game, were just as devoted to golf as their parishioners, but inhibited by their cloth from giving the same vent to their feelings. One unfortunate incumbent, suffering even worse form than usual, at length uttered an expression most unsuited to his calling and was properly rebuked by his partner, another minister.

"It's nae guid", he replied, "I'll juist hae to gie it up."

"What", said his horrified companion, "gie up gowf?"

"Nae, nae", was the reply, "gie up the kirk."

TOM SCOTT AND GEOFFREY COUSINS, *FROM "THE WIT OF GOLF"*

The golfer was transported to Heaven and found it was a magnificent golf course flanked by trees, like a celestial Pinehurst. With his angel guide he set out to explore and the first player he saw was shaping to cut the corner of a dogleg, a feat demanding a carry of at least three hundred yards.

"That shot will be a miracle", observed the newcomer, "who does he think he is – St Peter?"

"It happens to *be* St Peter", whispered the angel, "but he thinks he's Arnold Palmer."

TOM SCOTT AND GEOFFREY COUSINS, *FROM "THE WIT OF GOLF"*

THE FIRST TEE ... IS IN ITS USUAL STATE OF TENSION.

THE CONSTITUENTS OF HALF A DOZEN FOURBALLS STAND ABOUT, SWISHING THEIR DRIVERS, WAITING TO GET OFF.

THEY ARE ALL HANDICAP PLAYERS, AND LOOK LIKE IT. THAT IS, THEY WEAR CLOTHING SPECIFICALLY DESIGNED FOR THE GAME. ZIPPERED JACKETS WITH GUSSETS LET INTO THE BACK TO PROVIDE AN EASY MOVEMENT OF THE SHOULDERS. RUBBERIZED, WATERPROOF SHOES, FELT CAPS AND HAIRY JERSEYS....

THEY ARE JOINED BY A COMMON EMOTION. ACUTE ANXIETY.

THIS IS CAUSED BY THE FACT THAT THEY DON'T KNOW FROM ADAM WHAT'S GOING TO HAPPEN WHEN THEIR TURN COMES TO STRIKE OFF — WHEN THEY HAVE TO STEP UP ON TO THE TEE AND BALANCE THE BALL ON A PEG AND, IN DEATH-LIKE SILENCE, HAVE A RIGID WAGGLE OR TWO AND THEN, RATHER SUDDENLY, A BASH AT IT, WITH EVERYONE WATCHING....

THEY MAY HOOK IT, AS USUAL, INTO THE LONG AND TANGLED GRASS BEHIND THE THIRD GREEN AND LOSE A BRAND-NEW BALL FIRST CRACK OUT OF THE BOX WHILE THE NEXT TWO MATCHES PLAY THROUGH, GETTING THE DAY OFF TO A JAGGED START FROM WHICH IT WILL CERTAINLY NOT RECOVER.

PATRICK CAMPBELL,
FROM "PATRICK CAMPBELL'S GOLFING BOOK"

If God wants to produce the ideal golfer then He should create a being with a set of unequal arms and likewise legs, an elbow-free left arm, knees which hinge sideways and a ribless torso from which emerges, at an angle of 45 degrees, a stretched neck fitted with one colour-blind eye stuck firmly on the left side. And please God, let him be British.

CHRIS PLUMRIDGE, *FROM "ALMOST STRAIGHT DOWN THE MIDDLE"*

A very enthusiastic golfer has a friend who was a noted clairvoyant, and he was always badgering his friend to contact someone from the beyond to see whether there was a golf course in Heaven. If there was, he wanted to know what sort of sand was in the bunkers, which were the out-of-bounds holes, how difficult the course was, what was par, whether there was a grill room, a good pro's shop, and so on.

The clairvoyant eventually said that when he had his next seance he would make some inquiries. So he did that, and about three weeks later the keen golfer saw the clairvoyant and asked whether he had any news. "Yes," said the clairvoyant, "I have some good news and some bad news. The good news is that there is the most superb golf course in Heaven. It's beautiful. It has Bermuda grass on the fairways and Penn Cross on the greens, the most beautiful crushed marble in the bunkers.

There is a superb clubhouse with a grill room, a marvellous men's locker room, a splendid pro's shop, golf carts, etcetera. It is really tip top."

"That's great," said the golfer. "But what's the bad news?"

"I booked you a starting time for next Tuesday at 2 o'clock."

PETER ALLISS, FROM "BEDSIDE GOLF"

There are two things you can learn by stopping your backswing at the top and checking the position of your hands: how many hands you have, and which one is wearing the glove.

FROM "GOLF FOREVER, WORK WHENEVER", COMP. MICHAEL RYAN

Never try to keep more than 300 separate thoughts in your mind during your swing.

FROM "GOLF FOREVER, WORK WHENEVER", COMP. MICHAEL RYAN

You've just one problem. You stand too close to the ball – after you've hit it.

SAM SNEAD, *Advice to a Pupil*

The secret of good golf is to hit the ball hard, straight, and not too often.

FROM "GOLF FOREVER, WORK WHENEVER", COMP. MICHAEL RYAN

THE WHOLE BODY MUST TURN ON THE PIVOT OF THE HEAD OF THE RIGHT THIGH-BONE WORKING IN THE COTYLOIDAL CAVITY OF THE *OS INNOMINATUM* OR PELVIC BONE; THE HEAD, RIGHT KNEE AND RIGHT FOOT REMAINING FIXED, WITH THE EYES RIVETED ON THE BALL. IN THE UPWARD SWING, THE VERTEBRAL COLUMN ROTATES UPON THE HEAD OF THE RIGHT FEMUR, THE RIGHT KNEE BEING FIXED; AND AS THE CLUB-HEAD NEARS THE BALL, THE FULCRUM IS RAPIDLY CHANGED FROM THE RIGHT TO THE LEFT HIP, THE SPINE NOW ROTATING ON THE LEFT THIGH-BONE, THE LEFT KNEE BEING FIXED.... NOT EVERY PROFESSIONAL INSTRUCTOR HAS SUCCEEDED IN PUTTING BEFORE HIS PUPIL THE CORRECT STROKE IN GOLF IN THIS ANATOMICAL EXPOSITION. "JUIST SWOOP HER AWA', MAISTER," SAYS ONE INSTRUCTOR. "HIT UT, MON," SAYS ANOTHER. BOTH ARE RIGHT, BUT SUCH APPARENTLY DISCORDANT ADMONITIONS PUZZLE THE NEOPHYTE.

ARNOLD HAULTAIN

… before retiring it's obviously a good idea to get out the putter, and knock a few balls up and down the carpet.

There's a design of stripes on the carpet which, by a happy coincidence, clearly demonstrates whether or not the club-head is being taken back, and brought forward, square to the line of the tooth mug which has been placed on the floor in the opposite corner of the room. But, according to the stripes on the carpet, the club-head is coming back *outside* the line, while the follow-through finishes several inches to the left of the tooth mug, and must, indeed, have been doing so for years. It's still, however, only 9.15. There's ample time to work on it—

By 10 p.m. you're getting only one in six into the tooth mug, against a previous average as high as three. Also, the carpet is much faster than the greens are likely to be. You achieve the conviction that you're practising a putting stroke which will not only push it six inches to the right of the hole every time, but also leave it at least two yards short. Throw the putter back into the bag and get into bed and try to forget all about the stripes. Try, indeed, not to think about golf at all—

Five minutes later you're up, in bare feet and pyjamas, in front of the full-length mirror in the wardrobe, trying to see what it looks like if you really do pull the left hand *down* from the top of the swing, instead of shoving the right shoulder round. Suddenly, it feels right so you get the driver out of the bag and have a swish with it in front of the mirror and it demolishes an alabaster bowl concealing the light fitting in the ceiling. Clear it up and back into

bed and try to think of some reasonable
explanation for the chambermaid
in the morning—
By midnight there's been another putting
session – disastrous – and a spell of short
chips into the wastepaper basket two of
which, striking the door high up with an
incredibly loud bang, provoked a thunderous
and outraged knocking on the wall from the
man next door. Back into bed – the feet
are frozen – where you lie with the sheet
up to the eyes wondering if the whole
hotel has been roused and the
manager, in his dressing-gown,
will soon be in with a
policeman, and they'll find
you've smashed the
alabaster bowl and
knocked all the paint
off the door and there's no
explanation. None, except
perhaps that you're playing the
Championship – or at it.

PATRICK CAMPBELL,
FROM "PATRICK CAMPBELL'S GOLFING BOOK"

... you and I know we'd pay almost anything to instantly improve our play, so herein lies the answer. You'd think that would be impossible but it's not – thanks to the gadget, the gizmo, the gimmick.

Yes, brothers and sisters, the gadget will be our redeemer – all hail to the (latest) greatest invention of the age! Come bathe in the glory of the plastic panacea – the cure for all our ills – the one pure light in a world of golfing darkness. We seekers after redemption on the fairways are a strange mixture of the cynical and the credulous. We may mistrust advertising hype, we may ignore the kindly advice of a passing member of the club who plays off scratch and happens to notice one of the grosser errors in our swing. No – the words we treat as the true gospel have a wonderful simplicity and conviction:

"My mate says it's foolproof!"

TOM O'CONNOR,
FROM "ONE FLEW OVER THE CLUBHOUSE"

If you are unsure whether your clothing is suitable for wear on a golf course, ask yourself if it combines the minimum imaginable taste with the maximum possible discomfort.

FROM "GOLF FOREVER, WORK WHENEVER",
COMP. MICHAEL RYAN

The final step in equipping oneself for the game of golf, and at the same time, maximising one's image as a competent golfer, is wardrobe selection. In reviewing the ... apparel acquisition methodology [of the golfer], one will come to understand that a golfer's taste in fashion might more precisely be referred to as a taste for the absurd.

GEOFF HOWSON

No matter what calamities befall him in everyday life, the true hacker still needs the pressure and inconvenience of four hours of trudging in wind or rain or sleet or sun (or all of them at once), hacking at a white pellet that seems to have a mind of its own, and a lousy sense of direction.

TOM O'CONNOR, *FROM "ONE FLEW OVER THE CLUBHOUSE"*

Golf is essentially an exercise in masochism conducted out of doors; it affords opportunity for a certain swank, it induces a sense of kinship in its victims, and it forces them to breathe fresh air, but it is, at bottom, an elaborate and addictive rite calculated to drive them crazy for hours on end and send them straight to the whiskey bottle after that.

PAUL O'NEIL, *FROM "LIFE", JUNE 15, 1962*

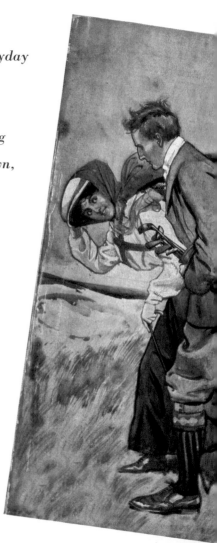

Have you ever noticed what golf spells backwards?

AL BOLISKA

… who would be mad enough to participate in this crazy ritual? Who would be so seriously maladjusted as to pay to be so punished mentally and physically? Who would? We would! Every time, every day if we could, every morning, every afternoon. When we see a pro make a mistake, we don't think pessimistically: "Well, if he can't do it, why am I bothering?" No, we exclaim, "Good heavens, you great pudd'n, I could do better than that!"

TOM O'CONNOR, *FROM "ONE FLEW OVER THE CLUBHOUSE"*

Golf – a game played by placing a small ball, 1½ inches in diameter, on top of a big ball, 8,000 miles in diameter, and trying to knock the small ball off the big ball rather than vice versa.

FRED BECK AND O.K. BARNES,
"73 YEARS IN A SAND TRAP"

Golf is a form of work made expensive enough for a rich man to enjoy it.

SEYMOUR DUNN,
FROM "THE COMPLETE GOLF JOKE BOOK"

Golf is a game whose aim is to hit a very small ball into a very small hole, with weapons singularly ill-designed for the purpose.

WINSTON CHURCHILL

Golf makes liars out of honest men, cheats out of altruists, cowards out of brave men and fools out of everybody.

MILTON GROSS

Golf is a game where when you don't succeed, you try, try again. And if you're honest, you mark it down on the score card.

SEYMOUR DUNN,
FROM "THE COMPLETE GOLF JOKE BOOK"

Golf is obsessional, vile, encourages gambling on the course and in the clubhouse, leads to bad language, the expenditure of a great deal of money (most of it wasted) and has wrecked many marriages. I cannot understand why anyone plays it. In fact the only reason I am spending my holidays golfing this year is because I'm convinced that with a bit of practice I can cure my hook. I'm sure I'm standing too close to the ball and relaxing the knees too much. I think that if I took up a more open stance and moved the front foot....

MICHAEL GREEN,
FROM "THE ART OF COARSE GOLF"

J.P.K., of Tacoma, Washington, passes along an old saw about a golf club whose members put on a banquet for the club's oldest golfer, on his hundredth birthday. The toastmaster spoke highly of the old man's well-preserved appearance, and spoke well, too, of his game. When the ancient golfer arose to speak, he said, "Fellow members, I will tell you the secret of my success. My wife and I were married seventy-eight years ago. On our wedding night we agreed that whenever we had an argument the one who was proved to be in the wrong would go out and play eighteen holes of golf. I have played this course daily, gentlemen, since 1877."

FRED BECK,
FROM "TO HELL WITH GOLF"

Caddies are a breed of their own. If you shoot sixty-six, they say, "Man, we shot sixty-six!" But go out and shoot seventy-seven, and they say, "Hell, he shot seventy-seven!"

LEE TREVINO

There are three classes of people who are entitled to refer to themselves as "We." They are Kings, Editors, and Caddies.

GERALD BATCHELOR

The professional cricketer can instruct an unskilled amateur, can take his ill-guarded wicket, and make him "give chances" all over the field, without bursting into yells of unseemly laughter. But the little caddie cannot restrain his joy when the tyro at golf, after missing his ball some six times, ultimately dashes off the head of his club against the ground. Nor is he less exuberant when his patron's ball is deep in a "bunker" or sand-pit, where the wretch stands digging at it with an iron – hot, helpless and wrathful.

ANDREW LANG

A parson at St Andrews, seeing a good drive fade into a bunker, stifled an unbecoming expression and instead muttered:

"Vade retro, Satanus."

"Nane o' that foreign swearing here", said the caddie, "Remember, ye're in Scotland."

TOM SCOTT AND GEOFFREY COUSINS,
FROM "THE WIT OF GOLF"

The caddies at St Andrews are a droll lot. Many of the older ones chafe a little under the new licence law. Their candour at times is remarkable. One day, one of them told his employer, in answer to a query about the golfing qualities of a prospective partner: "He canna play worth a d – n, sir; he's nae better than yerself."

MILES BANTOCK

A young player, wintering at Pau, in France, and almost wholly ignorant of the language, had for his caddie a French boy who knew no English. They managed to get on by the language of signs. At last the player made a remarkably good approach shot, and his ball lying dead, he turned round with an air of intense satisfaction and triumph to his caddie, who instantly exclaimed, "Beastly fluke!" It was all the English that he knew.

ANONYMOUS

One thing that's always available on a golf course is advice. If you play like I do, you think everybody knows something you don't know. If I see a bird fly over, I think he's going to tell me something.

BUDDY HACKETT

Asked for advice on how to hit the ball farther –
"Hit it a *!*#!! sight harder!"

TED RAY

Did you ever consider hitting it closer to the hole?

BEN HOGAN,
FROM "SPORTS ILLUSTRATED", 1975

There is no need to believe people who say they play golf for the fresh air and the exercise, the ones who tell you they just like to give it a good old bash and never mind who wins, the ones who assure you that they go out in hail, rain and snow just for the fun of it. All these people, every time they stand on the first tee, are expecting to play the round of their life. Pleasure lies in playing well, misery lies in scuffling it into the rough.

PATRICK CAMPBELL,
FROM "PATRICK CAMPBELL'S GOLFING BOOK"

The biggest liar in the world is the golfer who claims that he plays the game merely for exercise.

TOMMY BOLT

After hitting her ball into her bra: "I'll take a two stroke penalty, but I'll be damned if I'll play it where it lays".

ELAIN JOHNSON

... if we play brilliantly, our mouths go into overdrive and the world never hears the end of it. If we play badly, our brains go into overkill and make it the *worst* round the world has ever seen.

TOM O'CONNOR, *FROM "ONE FLEW OVER THE CLUBHOUSE"*

In golf, I'm one under. One under a tree, one under a rock, one under a bush....

GERRY CHEEVERS, *Former NHL Goalie*

These humiliations are the essence of the game.

ALISTAIR COOKE, *FROM "INSIDE GOLF"*

Golf should not be a battle in the lifemanship war, or a virility test, or a social asset or an excuse for gambling, or a character-building hobby, or a reason for not taking the family out on Sundays, although it may contain elements of all of them. Essentially it is for amusement only.

PETER DOBEREINER

The glorious thing is that thousands of golfers, in park land, on windy downs, in gorse, in heather, by the many-sounding sea, enjoy their imbecilities, revel in their infirmities, and from failure itself draw that final victory the triumph of hope.

R.C. ROBERTSON-GLASGOW

ONE PLAYER IN A THREE-BALL GAME WALKED INTO THE CLUBHOUSE LOOKING TIRED AND WORRIED AND TOLD THE SECRETARY THAT ONE OF HIS PARTNERS HAD COLLAPSED AND DIED AT THE 9TH HOLE, THE FARTHEST POINT ON THE COURSE.

"HOW TRAGIC", EXCLAIMED THE SECRETARY. "HOW CAN WE GET HIM BACK?"

"OH, WE'VE BROUGHT HIM BACK", SAID THE PLAYER, "WE JUST COULDN'T LEAVE HIM OUT THERE".

"THAT MUST HAVE BEEN FEARFULLY TIRING FOR YOU BOTH", OBSERVED THE SECRETARY.

"WELL IT WAS, BUT NOT THE CARRYING. THE TROUBLE WAS PUTTING HIM DOWN AND LIFTING HIM UP BETWEEN SHOTS."

TOM SCOTT AND GEOFFREY COUSINS, *FROM "THE WIT OF GOLF"*

ERIC: MY WIFE SAYS IF I DON'T GIVE UP GOLF; SHE'LL LEAVE ME.

ERNIE: THAT'S TERRIBLE.

ERIC: I KNOW – I'M REALLY GOING TO MISS HER.

ERIC MORECAMBE AND ERNIE WISE, *FROM "THE MORECAMBE AND WISE JOKE BOOK", 1979*

Golf appeals to the idiot in us and the child. What child does not grasp the simple pleasure-principle of miniature golf? Just how childlike golf players become is proven by their frequent inability to count past five.

JOHN UPDIKE

For most amateurs, the best wood in the bag is the pencil.

CHI CHI RODRIGUEZ

If you pick up a golfer and hold it close to your car, like a conch shell, and listen, you will hear an alibi.

FRED BECK

The only way of really finding out a man's true character is to play golf with him. In no other walk of life does the cloven hoof so quickly display itself.

P.G. WODEHOUSE

A golfer might as well turn in his clubs if he can't find some excuse for his own duffery.

MILTON GROSS

The only thing that counts in golf is the final number on the scorecard. I always keep my own score. I mark it correctly, to the best of my knowledge. But with all the strokes I take on a hole, I think I can be forgiven if I forget one … or two … but one time I went too far. I made a hole in one and marked down a zero.

BOB HOPE, *FROM "CONFESSIONS OF A HOOKER"*

*B*ut for sheer systematic nuttiness, nothing can compare with an annual ceremony put on by the Oxford and Cambridge Golfing Society, a collection of leather-elbowed oldsters and shaggy-haired youngsters who play for the President's Putter, no less, every year in the first week of January at Rye ... This tournament is intended to prove the English boast that "we can play golf every day of the year". If they can do it at Rye in January, they can do it at the South Pole, which in some sharp ways Rye resembles. At any rate, ... Snow, hail, wind, torrents – nothing can keep them from the swift completion of their Micklem-appointed rounds.

I was there four years ago. On the first morning, the small town and the course were completely obliterated in a fog denser than anything in Dickens. It seeped into the hotels so you needed a links boy to light your way to your plate of bacon, baps and bangers. I assumed the whole thing was off, till a telephone call warned a few dallying competitors that their

tee-off time was about to strike. We crawled out to the course, and the first person I ran into, marching around the clubhouse, was Micklem. I asked him if anyone was out there, and if so, why. "Nonsense," he barked. "they're all out there. Haven't lost a ball yet." He motioned toward the great grey nothingness outside, not fog, not landscape, but what John Milton (13 handicap) once called "not light but darkness visible"…

I hopped off into what might very well have been the edge of the world, as it was conceived by those Portuguese mariners who would have liked very much to discover America but who were afraid to sail out into the Atlantic, beyond sight of land, for fear of falling off. I ran into a swirl of nothingness and, sure enough, there emerged, like a zombie on the heath in a horror film, a plumpish, confident figure recognisable at three yards as Steel.

He took out an iron for his approach shot, though what he thought he was approaching I have no idea – San Salvador, no doubt. He hit it lowand clean, and a sizable divot sailed away from him and vanished. He went off after it and vanished too. I kept following in the gloom, and from time to time a wraith swinging a golf club would loom up, take two steps and be gone.

It was true! They all finished, and nobody lost a ball. I felt my way back to the clubhouse, and at the end the last ghost was in. Within five minutes they were up against the bar, chests out, faces like lobsters, beer mugs high, slapping thighs, yokking it up. Queer fish, the Oxford and Cambridge Golfing Society. They behave just as if they'd been out for a round of golf. What they play each year on that barren fork of Sussex that reaches out to the Channel, and Holland, and eventually to the Bering Strait, is a wholly new game: Invisible Golf.

ALISTAIR COOKE, *FROM "GOLF" MAGAZINE*

*My game is so bad I gotta hire three caddies –
one to walk the left rough, one for the right rough,
and one down the middle.
And the one in the middle doesn't have
to do very much at all.*

DAVE HILL

*I don't say my golf game is bad; but if I grew
tomatoes, they'd come up sliced.*

MILLER BARBER

*The first hole on the course was a short one, and the
novice was being instructed in the game by a friend.
Standing rather nervously he aimed a vicious swipe
at the ball, which was half-topped,
careered all the way to the green,
hit the flagstick and dropped in.
"That's done it!" he cried, "now I've
lost my ball!"*

TOM SCOTT AND GEOFFREY COUSINS,
FROM "THE WIT OF GOLF"

... the worse one is at golf, the more obsessional it becomes. It's a complete fallacy that it's the boys who are fifteen handicap who worry about getting down into single figures. They don't care a damn. It's the Coarse Golfer who becomes fixated, usually about breaking a hundred. He doesn't worry about having his handicap reduced – he just wants to get one. Even winning is secondary to getting round the course without disgracing himself and receiving pitying smiles.

MICHAEL GREEN, *FROM "THE ART OF COARSE GOLF"*

That elegant funny-man Dickie Henderson said he once played eighteen holes at Palm Springs with the legendary Arnold Palmer. As the round ended Dickie asked anxiously, "What do you think of my game?" Palmer said, "Not bad but I still prefer golf."

BOB MONKHOUSE

A beginner's golf game is improving when he is able to hit the ball in one.

FROM "GOLF FOREVER, WORK WHENEVER", COMP. MICHAEL RYAN

The Coarse Golfer: one who has to shout 'Fore' when he putts.

MICHAEL GREEN, *FROM "THE ART OF COARSE GOLF"*

The idea is to get the golf ball from a given point into each of the eighteen cups in the fewest strokes and the greatest number of words. The ball must not be thrown, pushed or carried. It must be propelled entirely by about $500 worth of curious looking implements especially designed to provoke the owner.

Each implement has a specific purpose and ultimately some golfers get to know what that purpose is. They are the exceptions.

After each hole has been completed the golfer counts his strokes. Then he subtracts six and says, "Made that in five. That's one above par. Shall we play for fifty cents on the next hole, too, Ed?" After the final, or eighteenth hole, the golfer adds up his score and stops when he has reached eighty-seven. He then has a swim, a pint of rye, sings "Sweet Adeline" with six or eight other liars and calls it the end of a perfect day.

ANONYMOUS

Soil flew in all directions as the novice attempted to tee off.

"I'm sure," he said to the caddie, "the worms will be worried!"

"Oh, no," replied the caddie. "The worms around here are very crafty. Most of them will be hiding under the ball for safety."

BOB EVANS

Golf develops a beginner's self-control, but caddying for a beginner develops it even more.

FROM "GOLF FOREVER. WORK WHENEVER", COMP. MICHAEL RYAN

I wasn't playing at my best the other day and the caddy I had was worse than useless. I said, "You must be the worst caddy in the world." And he said, "No, that would be too much of a coincidence." What do you tip a man like that? As I was leaving I said to the pro, "That caddy is a cheeky swine. You were watching my game – what do you think I should give him?" He said, "Your clubs."

BOB MONKHOUSE

Golfer in the woods: "Caddy, why are you looking at your watch?" Caddy: "That's no watch, it's a compass."

VIC FREDERICKS, FROM "FOR GOLFERS ONLY"

One of the club officials was making a
routine check of the course when he
came upon a golfer who was preparing
to drive a ball from a spot twenty feet
in front of the tee.
"Sir," he pointed out, "you can't drive
from there."
"Get lost," said the exasperated
swinger, "this is my fourth shot."

VIC FREDERICKS,
FROM "FOR GOLFERS ONLY"

...there's this term 'handicap player'
used disparagingly by golf writers to
mean someone who's no good.
They don't understand that to a
Coarse Golfer 'handicap player'
is a term of high praise – it means
someone who is actually good enough
to have a handicap.

MICHAEL GREEN,
FROM "THE ART OF COARSE GOLF"

Hook: the addiction of fifty percent
of golfers.
Slice: the weakness of the other half.

JIM BISHOP

"No man is a hero to his caddy"

DUDLEY DOUST

"Real golfers, whatever the
provocation, never strike a caddy with
the driver . . . The sand wedge is far
more effective."

ANONYMOUS

"The only time I talk on the golf course
is to my caddy, and only then to
complain."

SEVE BALLESTEROS

"My caddy."

WALTER TRAVIS, *about his handicap*

A game of golf is usually played between two, sometimes four, friends. Each player tries to urge his golf ball into a special hole in the grass by tapping it with one of his bundle of sticks. When the ball eventually drops into the hole the golfer remembers the number of whacks it took him and, if his friend is watching, writes that number down on his scorecard. After doing this 18 times the friends add up their scores to find the winner. As in receiving a prison sentence, or the news of a multiple birth of offspring, a low number is hoped for. After working out who is the winner, the losers all say "Well done!" and silently accompany their ex-friend back to the clubhouse.

FRANK MUIR, *FROM "ONE OVER PAR"*

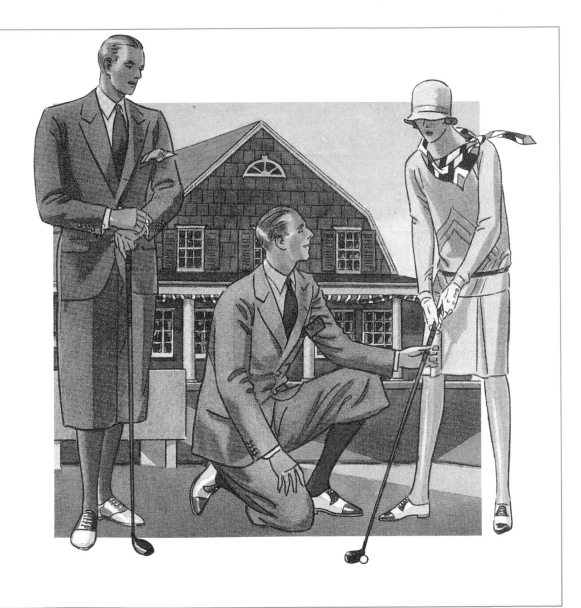

TEXT ACKNOWLEDGEMENTS

The publishers are grateful for permission to reproduce copyright material. Every effort has been made to trace copyright holders, but the publishers would be pleased to hear from any not here acknowledged.

PETER ALLISS: extracts from *"Bedside Golf"* and *"More Bedside Golf"*, 1984, published by Fontana, a division of HarperCollins Publishers Ltd.

FRED BECK: extracts from *"To Hell With Golf"*, published by Hill and Wang, 1956

PATRICK CAMPBELL: extracts from *"Patrick Campbell's Golfing Book"*, published by Blond and Briggs © Patrick Campbell 1963, 1972

ALISTAIR COOKE: extract from *"Golf"* magazine, taken from *"A Golfer's Companion"* ed. Chris Plumridge and John Hopkins

VIC FREDERICKS: extracts from *"For Golfers Only"*, published by Frederick Fell, New York

MICHAEL GREEN: extracts from *"The Art Of Coarse Golf"*, published by Hutchinson, © Michael Green 1967. Reprinted by permission of Richard Scott Simon Agency

GEOFF HOWSON: extracts from *" Golf: How To Look Good When You're Not"* published by Contemporary Books Inc., Chicago, © Geoff Howson 1988

RICHARD MINTZER: extracts from *"The Unofficial Golfer's Handbook"* published by Plume Books, a division of Penguin USA, 1991

BOB MONKHOUSE: extracts from *"Just Say A Few Words"*, published by Lennard Books Ltd., an imprint of Random House UK Ltd., © Bob Monkhouse 1988

FRANK MUIR: extract from *"One Over Par"* by Peter Alliss and Mike Seabrook, published by H.F and G.Witherby Ltd., a division of Cassell, 1992

ERIC NICOL and DAVE MORE: extracts from *"Golf - The Agony And The Ecstasy"* published by Robson Books Ltd., 1983

TOM O'CONNOR: extracts from *"One Flew Over The Clubhouse"*, published by Robson Books Ltd., 1993

MARK OMAN: extracts from *"Portrait Of A Golfaholic"* published by Contemporary Books Inc., Chicago, © Mark Oman 1985

CHRIS PLUMRIDGE: extracts from *"Almost Straight Down The Middle"*, published by Queen Anne Press/Lennard Associates Ltd., 1993

TOM SCOTT and GEOFFREY COUSINS: extracts from *"The Wit Of Golf"* published by Leslie Frewin Publishers, 1972

MIKE SEABROOK: extracts from *"One Over Par"* by Peter Alliss and Mike Seabrook, published by H.F and G.Witherby Ltd., a division of Cassell, 1992.

Extracts from *"Golf Forever, Work Whenever"* compiled by Michael Ryan, © 1993 The Great Quotations Publishing Company

PICTURE CREDITS

The publishers are very grateful to the following individuals & organisations for permission to reproduce their pictures. Whilst all reasonable efforts have been made to clear copyright and acknowledge sources and artists, Exley Publications would be happy to hear from any copyright holder who may have been omitted.

Front cover: © *1995 Sarah Baddiel, The Lynn Tait Gallery and Popperfoto. Title page and pages 10, 11, 14, 17, 20/21, 22, 27, 30, 32, 34/35, 36, 37, 38, 43, 46, 48/49, 50/5l, 60, 63, 64, 66/67, 69, 70/71, 73, 74/75, 78, 80, 81, 83, 84, 85, 87, 91:* © *l995 Sarah Fabian Baddiel, Golfiana, Grays in the Mews, B10 Davies Mews, London Wl, tel: 0171-408 1239. Page 8:* © *1995 Suyapa Quinn, The Image Bank. Page 12: Harper's Magazine 1898, Lords Gallery, London, The Bridgeman Art Library. Page 18: Paluan/Art Resource. Page 24: "Newton, Golfer and Caliper", Wally Neibart, The Image Bank. Page 29: "Devil Golf Ball" Wally Neibart, The Image Bank. Page 31: "Graphite Golf Club", Ann Meisel, The Image Bank. Page 41: Nick Birch. Page 52: "Punch" front cover, December 7, 1960. Page 58:* © *1995 The Royal Mail. Page 65: Russell Barnett. Page 76/77: "How can you detect your true golfer from your average man in the street?", William Heath Robinson, Chris Beetles Gallery, The Bridgeman Art Library. Page 86: "A Grand Match on St. Andrews Links", Charles Lees, Visual Arts Library. Page 88/89: "The Rules of Golf", The Lynn Tait Gallery. Pages 6, 23, 39, 44, 54/55, 72, 82: sources unknown.*